THE LITTLE TOFU BOOK

Linda Sonntag

PIATKUS

© 1987 Judy Piatkus (Publishers) Limited

First published in 1987 by
Judy Piatkus (Publishers) Limited,
5 Windmill Street, London W1P 1HF

British Library Cataloguing in Publication Data
The Little tofu book.
1. Cookery (Tofu)
I. Sonntag, Linda
641.6′5655   TX815.5.T63

ISBN 0-86188-680-1

Drawings by Trevor Newton
Designed by Susan Ryall
Cover illustrated by Hanife Hassan

Phototypeset in 10 on 11pt Linotron Plantin by
Phoenix Photosetting, Chatham
Printed and bound in Great Britain at
The Bath Press, Avon

CONTENTS

Dengaku, Japanese
country-style tofu
spread with miso.

WHAT IS TOFU?

Tofu has become the wonderfood of the 1980s in the West, but in the Orient it has formed a staple part of the diet of millions of people for thousands of years. Tofu is the Japanese word for beancurd. It is made from soya beans, which means that it is high in protein, low in calories and very cheap. In fact it is the cheapest and richest source of protein available in the world.

In the East, tofu shops are as common as bakers are in the West. The tofu master and his wife rise at dawn to prepare fresh tofu daily and it is sold in huge quantities – some families eat it three times a day. In the past decade tofu has caught on in Britain and America among healthfood eaters and lovers of Oriental cuisine to such an extent that new firms have been set up to produce it locally. Tofu is still imported from Japan – 'Morinaga' silken tofu in longlife tetrapacks is the most common Japanese variety available here – but increasingly fresh tofu is appearing in good delicatessens and healthfood shops.

If you have never tried tofu before, you may be baffled by its appearance, as it is like no other food on earth. It is sold in packs of about 8oz/225g. It is creamy white and comes in three different consistencies: silken tofu, which is like barely set custard; regular or medium tofu, which is soft but can be cut with a knife into cubes; and firm tofu, which as the name implies is solid enough to be held up by a corner of the block without breaking. Each of these types can be used in a variety of ways.

Tofu has a delicate taste and absorbs other flavours easily. It can be eaten on its own, but is almost always marinated, perhaps just in soy sauce, perhaps in a combination of condiments including chillies, lemon juice, garlic, oil, sherry (or Japanese sake) or ginger, so that it acts as a vehicle for these flavours. It needs very little cooking – no more than heating through.

Thus it is a very versatile ingredient and can be added to many dishes containing meat, fish, seafood, eggs and vegetables. In China it is often used as an extender for meat, and during the Ming Dynasty (1368–1644) it was known as 'young lamb' because of its tenderness and wholesomeness. The recipes in this book are purely vegetarian.

Cooks in Britain and America have discovered that tofu can be adapted wonderfully to Western cooking. The silken variety can be blended with other ingredients to make drinks, dressings, dips, spreads, desserts, quiches, sauces and soups. The regular and firm types can be cubed, marinated, lightly cooked and added to salads, casseroles, vegetable, egg and grain dishes, or deep-fried or barbecued and eaten with a spicy sauce.

Because it is nutritious and easily digestible, tofu can be enjoyed by babies and invalids; and because it is high in protein and low in calories it can become a key slimmer's food. Its versatility means that it can be eaten at any meal by any member of the family.

STORING TOFU

Morinaga silken tofu will keep without refrigeration for six months. Other varieties are best eaten as fresh as possible.

The average serving per person of regular or firm tofu is 2oz/50g, and if you have any left over it can be stored for two or three days in a bowl of water in the fridge. The water should be changed every day, as it gets cloudy and the tofu starts to ferment. If it has been kept for too long the tofu will be slimy to the touch and give off a not unpleasant citrus sort of smell. At this stage it is considered a delicacy in some parts of the world, but the taste for smelly tofu has not yet caught on in the West. Slightly overripe tofu can be rescued by parboiling.

Spreads and dips made with tofu can be stored in screw-topped jars for about a week in the fridge. Deep-fried tofu will keep for up to 10 days and can be reheated by steaming or lightly shallow-frying.

WHAT TO DO WITH TOFU

The most popular ways of cooking tofu – in the West as in the East – are shallow-frying and deep-frying. Shallow-fried tofu is often marinated first. Deep-fried tofu can be coated in a flavoured batter or served with a savoury dip. It is best to use firm or medium tofu for frying. On Morinaga silken tofu packets it says that you can slice and fry the contents, but silken tofu is in fact too sloppy for this. However, if you can't buy a firmer variety, silken tofu can be firmed up.

TO FIRM UP TOFU

Wrap the block in a clean cloth, preferably muslin, and stand it on a wire rack over a bowl in the fridge so that moisture can drain from it. Alternatively, leave the wrapped tofu on a chopping board slanting towards the sink. If you want to firm up regular tofu for frying, half an hour should suffice. Silken tofu should be drained for 24 hours, when it will be firm enough to cut.

TO PRESS TOFU

To make it firmer still, wrap the tofu in muslin or a clean cloth and put a weight on top of it to squeeze out excess liquid. Leave it somewhere where it can drain, such as in a margarine tub with holes punched in it. Or cube or slice the tofu first, then wrap and weight in a colander.

TO SQUEEZE TOFU

To give tofu the consistency of cottage cheese, squeeze it in a cloth until crumbly. Use it just like cottage cheese, on its own or mixed with diced fruit or vegetables.

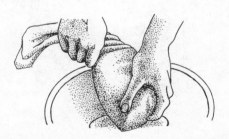

To Blend Tofu

Silken tofu is the easiest type to use when making sauces, dips, spreads and creamy desserts. If using firmer tofu, chop it up first and, to avoid straining the motor of your blender, put any liquid ingredients in the blender with the tofu. Tofu can also be mashed with a fork or a pastry blender.

To Steam Tofu

Put the tofu cubes or slices on a trivet over boiling water for a couple of minutes to heat them through. If you don't want to use oil for frying, they will heat through with no loss of nutrients.

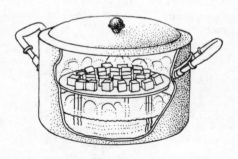

To Parboil Tofu

There are three reasons why you might want to do this.
* To heat it up for eating with a sauce.
* To firm it up.
* To freshen it up if you've kept it just a little too long.

Bring a pan of water to the boil, add the tofu and bring back to the boil. Take the pan off the heat and let it stand, covered, for 2 minutes.

To Scramble Tofu

Put the tofu in a pan without any oil over a gentle heat. Break it up with a wooden spoon or spatula. Cook for about 5 minutes, then drain and cool. This will give a drier version of the cottage cheese-type product obtained by squeezing.

To Freeze Tofu

If you freeze tofu it turns brown and its consistency becomes spongy and meaty. Defrost it and use instead of meat in casseroles and sandwiches. Do not attempt to deep-fry tofu after it has been frozen, as it is so absorbent that it will soak up the oil.

To Dry Tofu

To make home-processed soya protein or meat substitute, first freeze tofu to give it the right meaty colour and texture. Defrost and press to extract as much moisture as possible. Season with soy sauce to give a meaty flavour, then dry on a baking sheet in a very low oven with the door ajar. Allow to cool, then crumble if liked (for substitute mince) and store indefinitely in an airtight container. Add dried to soups and casseroles instead of meat.

To reconstitute for use in other dishes, such as stir-fries, mix the soya protein with an equal quantity of water and let it stand for 20 minutes. It should absorb all the water and regain a meaty texture.

8

TOFU RECIPES

PUMPKIN SOUP WITH TOFU CUBES

Fried tofu cubes can be used instead of croûtons on top of soups as well as in salads.

2 tablespoons oil or polyunsaturated margarine
1 onion, sliced
8 oz (225g) potatoes, peeled and cubed
1 lb (450g) pumpkin, skin and seeds removed, cubed
2 pints (1 litre) water
salt and pepper to taste
4 oz (100g) tofu, cubed
1 tablespoon soy sauce
1 tablespoon sesame seeds
4 sprigs basil or parsley

Heat the oil or margarine in a deep pan, add the onion and sweat until transparent. Add the potatoes, pumpkin and water, cover and cook gently for 20 minutes, or until the potato is soft. Blend the soup and add salt and pepper to taste.

Marinate the tofu in the soy sauce for 5 minutes, then heat through gently in a pan with a little oil.

Divide the soup between four bowls, spoon the tofu croûtons on top, sprinkle with sesame seeds and add a sprig of basil or parsley to garnish.

Serves 4

TOFU-TOPPED PIZZA

Squeezed tofu is mixed with crushed garlic, parmesan cheese, olive oil and basil to give a tofu version of pesto, which tastes lovely on top of a pizza with black olives. This recipe makes two 7 inch (18 cm) pizzas.

For the pizza dough
1/2 oz (15g) fresh yeast or 1/4 oz (7g) dried yeast
1 teaspoon sugar
1/4 pint (150ml) tepid water
7 oz (200g) plain white flour
pinch of salt

For the topping
2 cloves garlic, crushed
8 oz (225g) tofu, squeezed (see p. 5)
2 tablespoons grated parmesan cheese
2 tablespoons olive oil
4 tablespoons chopped basil leaves
2 oz (50g) pitted black olives, sliced

For the dough, put the yeast and sugar in 2 tablespoons of the water and leave for 10 minutes until frothy.

Sieve the flour into a warm bowl with the salt. Make a well in the centre, add the yeast mixture and the remaining liquid. Mix together to form a pliable dough, turn out on to a floured board and knead for about 5 minutes until smooth. Put the dough in a bowl, cover with a damp cloth and leave in a warm place to rise until doubled in size (about an hour).

Knead again for a couple of minutes, then divide in two and roll each half into a circle. Preheat the oven to 450°F/230°C/Gas 8.

Put the pizzas on an oiled baking sheet and crimp the edges slightly to hold in the filling.

Pound together all the ingredients for the topping (except the olives) in a mortar with a pestle. Spread over the topping and arrange the olive slices on top. Bake for 5 minutes, then reduce the heat to 400°F/200°C/Gas 6 and bake for a further 10 minutes.

Sprinkle a little more olive oil over the tops of the pizzas and serve hot.

Serves 2 or 4 depending on appetites

TOFU AND SPINACH LAYERED PANCAKES

This is a delicious combination of fillings. Roll the pancakes up to eat individually, or for a more spectacular looking dish, layer them and cut like a cake. For a change, try these fillings layered between leaves of filo pastry and baked in the oven.

For the batter
6 oz (175g) untreated white flour
pinch of salt (optional)
2 eggs
¾ pint (450ml) soya or dairy milk
1 tablespoon oil

For the spinach filling
2 lbs (1kg) spinach
8 oz (225g) tofu, scrambled (see p. 7)
nutmeg to taste

For the tomato filling
1 tablespoon oil
1 medium onion, chopped
1 clove garlic, chopped
15 oz (400g) canned tomatoes, drained and chopped
1 tablespoon tomato purée
2 teaspoons fresh oregano, chopped
salt (optional)
freshly ground black pepper

To make the batter, sift the flour with the salt into a bowl, make a well in the middle and break in the eggs. Add the milk slowly, beating to break the eggs, and gradually incorporate the flour. When half the milk has been added, beat in the oil. Add the remaining milk until the batter reaches the consistency of thin cream. Leave to stand for about 30 minutes.

Meanwhile, prepare the fillings. Cook the spinach and drain very well, squeezing all the water out with the back of a wooden spoon. (Save the spinach liquor and drink it, or add to stock or soup.) Chop the spinach and mix with the tofu. Season with a little grated nutmeg.

Heat the oil and sweat the onion and garlic until soft. Mix in the tomatoes and tomato purée, and bubble until thick. Stir in the herbs and season.

Make the pancakes in the traditional way.

Assemble the dish, layering the pancakes first with spinach, then with tomato filling. Cut like a cake to serve.

Serves 4

CURRIED TOFU AND MUSHROOMS

Although it is not a food found in India, tofu is very good in curries because of its ability to absorb both delicate and strong flavours. Use it in place of fish or add to vegetable curries, remembering that it won't need more than a few minutes cooking. Serve this as a side dish.

1 onion, chopped
1 clove garlic, crushed
1 teaspoon turmeric
1/2 teaspoon chilli powder
1/2 teaspoon salt (optional)
2 tablespoons oil
1/2 onion, sliced
12 oz (350 g) mushrooms, sliced
8 oz (225g) tofu, cubed
lime or lemon juice

Pound together the onion, garlic, turmeric, chilli powder and salt to form a paste. Heat the oil in a pan and fry the paste for 1 minute.

Add the sliced onion and mushrooms and fry until nearly done. Keep stirring while they soften. Add the tofu cubes and continue to cook for 2–3 minutes.

Serve sprinkled with lime or lemon juice.

Serves 4

TOFU CHILLI

Make this dish with fresh tofu, or use reconstituted frozen and dried tofu (see page 8) for a meaty taste.

8 oz (225g) tofu, cubed
few drops chilli sauce (natural product, bottled) or ½ teaspoon chilli powder
1 teaspoon ground cumin
¼ teaspoon cayenne pepper
1–2 tablespoons oil
1 leek, sliced and 1 onion, chopped
1 stick celery, sliced
1 clove garlic, crushed
4 oz (100g) mushrooms, sliced
14 oz (400g) canned tomatoes, chopped, with juice
1 tablespoon tomato purée
14 oz (400g) canned red kidney beans, drained

Marinate the tofu in a little chilli sauce (it is *very* hot) with the cumin and cayenne pepper. If using chilli powder, mix it with some of the juice from the canned tomatoes.

Meanwhile, heat the oil in a large saucepan, add the leek, onion, celery and garlic and sweat until soft. Add the mushrooms. When they are soft and juicy, stir in the tomatoes, tomato purée and beans. Heat through for 5 minutes, stirring. Add the tofu and marinade and cook for a further 2–3 minutes. Serve with rice or a baked potato and green salad.

Serves 4

Spring Vegetable Hotpot With Tofu

The fresh taste of tender young vegetables combines with soya-flavoured tofu cubes to produce a delicious, nutritionally complete meal. No extra salt is necessary because both the soy sauce and the miso contain salt.

1½ lbs (675g) new potatoes
fresh mint
6 oz (175g) baby carrots
6 oz (175g) broad beans
4 oz (100g) mangetout peas
4 oz (100g) garden peas
6 oz (175g) tofu cubes, marinated in soy sauce
1 teaspoon miso (see page 56)

Boil the potatoes in their skins with a sprig of mint until tender.

Meanwhile, sweat the carrot with very little water in a large closed pan over low heat. Open the pan occasionally to check that the water has not evaporated, and add the remaining vegetables when the carrots are about half cooked.

Add the tofu cubes and cooked potatoes about 3 minutes before the end of cooking time. Then drain the vegetables and reserve the water. Combine this water with the miso, pour over the vegetables and sprinkle on some chopped mint.

Serves 4

Ratatouille Tart

If you have some leftover ratatouille this is a good way of making it go further. You can use tofu in any suitable quiche recipe instead of béchamel sauce or cream and eggs.

8 oz (225g) ratatouille (made from a selection of the
following vegetables: onion, garlic, aubergine, cour-
gettes, mushrooms, peppers, canned tomatoes)
8 oz (225g) silken tofu
8 inch (20cm) wholemeal pastry case

To make the ratatouille, first cube the aubergine, put in a colander and sprinkle with salt; leave to drain. Slice the onion and garlic and fry in a little oil until transparent. Add the sliced and deseeded peppers, close the pan and cook for 5 minutes. Add the remaining vegetables, including the rinsed aubergines and the tomatoes chopped with their juice. Simmer gently until all the vegetables are soft and the flavours have mingled (30–40 minutes). Meanwhile, preheat the oven to 375°F/190°C/Gas 5.

Mix the ratatouille with the tofu and fill the pastry case with it. Bake for 25 minutes and serve with salad.

Serves 4–8

RASPBERRY TOFU CHEESECAKE

This delicious refrigerator cheesecake is much lower in calories than the traditional type.

For the base
4 oz (100g) butter
8 oz (225g) wholemeal biscuits, crushed

For the filling
1 sachet gelatine
6 tablepoons warm water
12 oz (350g) tofu
10 oz (275g) yoghurt
2 oz (50 g) cream cheese
4 tablespoons runny honey
2 oz (50 g) raspberries

To decorate
whole raspberries

To make the base: Melt the butter over a gentle heat, remove from the heat and stir in the crumbs. Use to line a 10 inch (26 cm) pie dish, pressing well down. Bake for 5 minutes at 325°F/160°C/Gas 3.

Dissolve the gelatine in the water. Combine the remaining ingredients in the blender until smooth, then add the melted gelatine. Pour into the crumb base and chill for 5 hours or overnight.

Decorate with whole raspberries and serve.

Serves 8–10

QUICK GRAPE DELIGHT

If you keep a packet of silken tofu in the cupboard, you will always have the basis of a quick creamy pudding to hand.

8 oz (225g) silken tofu
4 tablespoons honey
6 oz (175g) grapes, halved and pitted
2 oz (50g) slivered almonds

Blend the tofu with the honey in a liquidizer and stir in most of the grapes and almonds. Divide between four sundae dishes, decorate with the remaining fruit and nuts and chill for half an hour before serving.

Serves 4

TOFU MILK SHAKES

In a blender, combine equal weights of tofu and soft fruit, adding enough milk – soya or dairy – to give the right consistency. Drop some shattered ice into the blender or, better still, use frozen fruit such as strawberries or raspberries. Desiccated coconut and slivered almonds add extra taste and texture. Omit the milk for a smooth creamy dessert.

DIPS AND SPREADS

Tofu lends itself perfectly to making all sorts of dips and spreads because of its readiness to absorb other flavours. Morinaga silken tofu is ideal for making anything with a creamy consistency. If using firmer tofu, cut it up into small pieces first.

Store the spread in a screw-topped jar in the fridge and eat with wholemeal bread, hot pitta bread, crunchy vegetables or baked potatoes.

To savoury dips you can add, say, chilli or tomato sauce; to sweet ones molasses or maple syrup. Combinations of vegetables, herbs, fruit, nuts and spices are endless. Here are a few suggestions.

CRUNCHY VEGETABLE SPREAD

8 oz (225g) tofu
4 oz (100g) carrots, finely diced
1 stick celery, finely chopped
1/3 cucumber, chopped
2 gherkins, chopped
1 tablespoon parsley, chopped
celery seeds to taste

Blend the ingredients together until the desired consistency is reached.

WATERCRESS DIP

8 oz (225g) tofu
1 bunch watercress, trimmed and chopped
a few black olives, pitted and chopped
1/2 red pepper, chopped

Blend the ingredients together until the desired consistency is reached.

HERB AND GARLIC DRESSING

4 oz (100g) tofu
2–3 tablespoons fresh herbs, chopped
1 small clove of garlic, crushed
1 tablespoon lemon juice
salt and pepper, if liked

Blend all the ingredients together, using as many different herbs as you like. Heated, this makes a good sauce for pasta, vegetables or fish. It will be quite garlicky.

Gazpacho Spread

8 oz (225g) tofu
1/2 green pepper, chopped
1/2 red pepper, chopped
1/2 medium onion, finely chopped
small clove of garlic, crushed
2–3 teaspoons tomato concentrate

Blend the ingredients together to the desired consistency.

Fruit And Nut Spread

6 oz (175g) dried figs
apple and cinnamon tea (or other herbal tea)
8 oz (225g) tofu
2 tablespoons apple purée
1–2 tablespoons cashew nuts
pinch of cinnamon
1–2 tablespoons honey

Stew the figs gently in the tea until plump and juicy. Chop them up. Reserve the juice.

Blend the figs with the ingredients to the desired consistency, adding some of the reserved juice if liked. Eat this creamy dessert with crisp biscuits.

TOFU, THE WONDER HEALTH FOOD

The Japanese suffer less from heart disease, high blood pressure and overweight than any other industrialised nation – a surprising fact given their stressful lifestyle. There is a Japanese saying: 'You are what you eat', and the number of strapping nonagenarians in the country certainly seems to indicate that the Japanese know what is good for them!

Tofu, rice and miso (see page 56) are the three foods most often eaten in the average Japanese household. Indeed it is quite likely that they will appear at every meal. The combination is as nutritious as it is delicious, because the soya foods tofu and miso contain amino acids that are not present in rice, and which are needed to activate its full nutritional potential. When these foods are eaten together the amount of available protein in the dish is increased by 30–40 per cent. Tofu and miso together provide protein and flavour, and the rice provides the fibre and texture in a perfectly balanced meal.

Tofu is a complete protein food because it contains all the eight essential amino acids. Protein is made up of 22 amino acids, and all but eight of them can be manufactured by the body from combinations of the others. The eight unique amino acids, which the body must get directly from its food supply, are present in tofu. In addition, it is a rich source of vitamins and minerals, containing B and E vitamins, choline, iron, potassium and phosphorus. Amazingly, it also contains more calcium than cows' milk!

Tofu itself contains no fibre – the fibrous bean pulp, called okara (see page 34), is left behind in the production of tofu and eaten as a food in its own right.

Tofu, on the other hand, is 95 per cent digestible, which means not only that the body gets maximum benefit from the nutrients it contains, but that it is good for babies and invalids and other people who literally cannot stomach beans. Soya beans themselves are only 68 per cent digestible, and it is of course the fibre in them, working its way through the gut, that causes flatulence, the bane of the bean-eater's life. Tofu-eaters are spared this embarrassment. And tofu is an alkaline food, which means that it is kind on the stomach anyway.

Another big health bonus for tofu is that it is low in saturated fats and contains absolutely no cholesterol, which makes it an ideal protein food for anyone who wants to reduce the risk of heart disease, one of the major killers in the West.

It is high in linoleic acid, an essential fatty acid not synthesised by the body, and in lecithin, which builds the tissues of the nerves and the brain.

As if this were not enough, this wonder health food is extremely low in calories, making it a must for slimmers (see page 29).

BROWN RICE, TOFU AND VEGETABLES

The addition of a tasty miso sauce makes this a meal that looks as appetising as it is healthy.

8 oz (225g) long-grain brown rice
2 tablespoons oil
2 spring onions, chopped
1 red pepper, sliced
2 stalks celery, sliced
4 oz (100g) French beans, cut into manageable lengths
4 oz (100g) sweetcorn kernels, or baby sweetcorn
8 oz (225g) tofu, cubed
1 tablespoon miso
2 tablespoons hot water

Cook the rice in boiling water until tender (30–40 minutes).

About 10 minutes before the rice is ready, heat the oil in a large pan or a wok and add the spring onions, red pepper and celery. After about 3 minutes, add the beans and sweetcorn. Stir-fry until nearly done, then add the tofu cubes.

Cream the miso in a cup with the hot water. Combine the cooked rice and vegetables and stir in the miso sauce. Serve immediately with soy sauce if liked.

Serves 4

THE FOOD FOR THE FUTURE

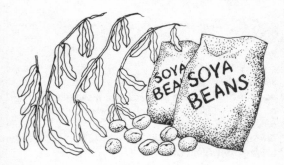

Tofu and its soya relative tempeh (see page 50) have been seen in the United States as heralding the most important diet revolution since the introduction of yoghurt. At first these new foods were produced only by small communities of people dedicated to a simple life, but now they are mass-produced and on sale in every foodstore and supermarket.

America, with its vast areas of grazing land, is traditionally a steak-eating nation, yet it is also the world's largest producer of soya beans. In America, as nowhere else, the battle rages: beef versus beans. People who are concerned about feeding the world argue that the soya bean yields 33 per cent more protein per acre than any other crop grown on this planet – 20 times as much protein as land used to raise cattle. They point out that it takes 15 lb cereal protein feed to yield 1 lb beef protein, and that the rich nations of the world use as much cereal to feed animals as the poor nations use to feed themselves. And they say that for the food cost of one steak, you could feed a whole restaurant full of hungry people with cereal protein.

It is not just the extravagance of rearing beef cattle for the world's richest people while millions starve that bothers the nutritionists. They are concerned that much of the soya protein available today is being wasted. Instead of being turned into tofu and tempeh, which could form a healthy replacement for meat in the diet of millions and provide millions more with the protein they lack altogether, 90 per cent of the soya beans grown in America for the domestic market are pressed to make oil. There is no protein in soya oil – it is all left behind in the bean pulp or presscake. And guess who gets to eat the presscake – the cattle.

Ecologists are also on the side of the bean, because it provides the land with free fertilizer. Soya beans, like all legumes, feed the soil with nitrogen. In the past, legumes were grown in rotation with other crops to regenerate the soil so that it in turn could feed the next crop grown on it – nitrogen is the main component in protein, and for a crop to be high in protein it must be grown in soil rich in nitrogen. But now that farmers no longer rotate their crops they have to use chemical fertilizers to ensure the harvest yields enough protein. They treat the soil with ammonium nitrate. The chemical residue from this fertilizer seeps away and is gradually polluting our water supplies.

Where soya beans are grown, the land gets all the nitrogen it needs; there is no pollution. And after the bean has been harvested the green plants can be used to make valuable organic compost.

It used to be thought that soya beans could only be cultivated in hot and humid countries – such as China, where gardening notes dating from 2000 BC show that the Chinese were already soya experts 4,000 years ago. But new strains have been developed and soya can now be grown successfully in most parts of the world.

The King of the Beans, known in the East as 'the meat of the soil' and regarded by the yogis as one of the five sacred grains, could be the answer to the world's famine problems. You could grow it in your garden at home, and make your own organic tofu.

TOFU FOR SLIMMERS

The fact that tofu is highly nutritious while being very low in calories makes it an excellent food for slimmers. It has only 13 calories per ounce (25g), and 2 oz (50g) is usually sufficient per serving. Below is a chart showing the calorie-counts of other high protein foods.

Food	Calories per ounce (25g)
Bacon, fried	169
Beans, baked	26
Beef, steak, grilled	86
Beefburger	70
Cashew nuts	178
Cheese, Cheddar	120
cottage	33
Chicken, roast	29
Cod, fried in batter	58
Egg, boiled	55
Kippers, grilled	31
Lamb chop, fried	146
Pork, roast	129

Tofu is clearly a top priority for weight-watchers, having less than half the calories of the traditional slimmer's favourite, cottage cheese. There is no reason why you shouldn't eat a lot of tofu without getting bored, as people tend to do on diets that centre around one food. Tofu is versatile, combines well with other low-calorie foods, such as fruit and vegetables, and absorbs other flavours, making it a different taste sensation every time. The fact that it is so quick to prepare is an added bonus and could stop the hungry dieter reaching for a forbidden biscuit instead of eating a proper meal.

Here is a sample low-calorie one-day menu with tofu in different guises. The recipes in the rest of the book will give you other ideas.

BREAKFAST

TOFU FRUIT CUP Blend 3 oz (75g) tofu in the liquidizer with 2 oz (50g) strawberries. Serve with 3 oz (75g) mixed fresh fruit (pineapple, melon, grapes, cherries or mandarin oranges).

LUNCH

SPINACH AND TOFU SALAD Marinate 2 oz (50g) tofu cubes in a few drops of chilli sauce. Shred 4 oz (100g) young spinach leaves, mix with: 1 spring onion, chopped; 2 small tomatoes, sliced; 3 mushrooms, sliced; ¼ cucumber, sliced. Make a dressing with 2 tablespoons natural yoghurt and a dash of chilli sauce and toss in the salad. Add the tofu cubes and serve.

SUPPER

TOFU CHOPS Drain and squeeze 4 oz (100g) regular tofu, then knead in a bowl for 5 minutes. Mix in 1 clove garlic, crushed; 2 spring onions, finely chopped, and 1 tablespoon chopped fresh herbs, such as parsley or basil. Knead again, until the tofu is doughy. Shape into two 'chops' and roll in wholemeal flour or breadcrumbs. Fry lightly in vegetable oil until hot through and crisp on the outside and serve with steamed broccoli.

MAKING YOUR OWN TOFU

Making your own tofu is as satisfying as baking your own bread – for taste, texture and freshness, shop-bought varieties just can't compare. And of course nothing can match the pleasure of eating home-produced food.

Tofu is not difficult to make, but as with baking bread, you need to develop a knack that comes with understanding the different stages of production. The great tofu masters of Japan say that after decades of making tofu they may still hit the peak of perfection only once in 20 batches – their senses are obviously tuned into tofu at a pitch outside the range of normal mortals. It takes about an hour to make, but allow time for the beans to soak first and for the tofu to settle afterwards.

Basically, tofu is made like this: soya beans are soaked, then ground. The purée is boiled and strained to produce soya milk. A coagulant is added to the milk to make it curdle – what you are aiming at is, after all, beancurd or bean cheese. The curds are spooned into a mould and pressed and a block of home-made tofu is born.

A great bonus when making tofu yourself is that you produce several other foods on the way, and there is absolutely no wastage. The bean purée is called *go*. The pulp that is left behind when the milk is drawn off is called *okara*. Even the *whey* that drains off the curds has its uses. *Soya milk* can be used in place of dairy milk for drinking and in recipes, and it can also be made into *yuba*.

The ingredients you will need to make tofu are soya beans, water and a coagulant. The natural coagulant used in Japan is called nigari – it is a seawater product and comes in the form of granules. It is available in this country in Oriental shops and your healthfood stockist will usually be pleased to order it for you if it is not already on the shelves. If you can't get nigari you can substitute the same amount of Epsom salts or use 1½ tablespoons lemon juice or cider vinegar. However, the resulting tofu will be much more soft and crumbly. Nigari is very reliable and produces the best, firmest tofu.

As for equipment, you will need large saucepans, a colander, a blender, muslin cloths and, to shape the tofu cake, a box with holes in it and a lid that fits just inside the rim so that it can be weighted down. The Japanese use specially made wooden boxes, but a margarine box with holes punched in it and the rim cut off the lid will do just as well.

THE METHOD

1. Soak 12 oz (350g) soya beans overnight in plenty of water, bearing in mind that they double in size. Use fresh beans, i.e. less than a year old.

2. Rinse and drain the beans, then purée each cup of beans with 1 pint (600 ml) hot water. You now have a slurry or mealy broth called go.

3. Tip the go into 2 pints (1.2 litres) boiling water, bring back to the boil and boil for 20 minutes, stirring occasionally. Break up the foam that builds up on top with a wooden spoon, or flick cold water at it to make it subside.

4. Put a muslin cloth inside the colander over a large pan. Pour the go into the muslin and press on the contents to squeeze through. Take up the corners of the cloth (wear rubber gloves, it will be hot), and force out as much liquid as you can. You now have okara in the bag and soya milk in the pan. Put the okara to one side to use later.

5. Bring the soya milk to the boil, stirring constantly. Take off the heat.

6. In a cup, mix 1 heaped teaspoon nigari with a little boiling water. Add this to the soya milk gradually, stirring all the time.

7. Cover the pan and leave for about 3 minutes for curds to form. You now have curds and whey.

8. Put a piece of muslin in the pressing box, and put the box in the colander over a clean pan. Spoon the curds into the box, cover the top with muslin, put on the lid and weight. Keep the whey that drains off.

9. Leave for an hour or so. Unwrap the block of fresh tofu under cold water. It should be medium-firm. You can eat it straight away or store it under cold water in the fridge, and use it for any of the recipes in this book.

THE BONUSES OF MAKING TOFU

There are five other foods associated with the tofu-making process, and each can be used in its own right.

GO

This is the slurry, the mixture of ground soya beans and boiling water cooked to a broth. It can be added to soups and casseroles as a thickener, made into croquettes and used to fortify puddings and breads.

In Japan it is often used to fortify miso soup. Simply add the cooked go to one of the soups on page 59 before putting in the miso. It will produce a thicker soup that can be eaten as a meal in itself.

OKARA

Okara is the soya bean pulp which remains behind when the beans are boiled, crushed and strained. On no account should it be discarded. It is important in the diet because of its fibre. It has slightly less than half the protein of tofu, less than half the fat and even fewer calories. It contains a little less iron than a hamburger, no sodium, twice the potassium of tofu and some B vitamins.

Okara has a nutty flavour and can be seasoned and cooked with vegetables, which is the traditional

Japanese way of eating it. It can also be dried and crumbled, when it will keep for three weeks in an airtight container. Okara can be used to make burgers, sausages and cakes. In the East it is also eaten by nursing mothers to enrich their milk. It is used for curing diarrhoea and for polishing woodwork.

SOYA BEAN MILK

Soya bean milk was drunk long before the birth of Christ. It can be made into cheese and yoghurt. More usefully, perhaps, exquisite drinks can be made with soya milk and crushed berries, fruit juices, herbs, nuts, coconut and honey. It can be carbonated with soda water.

Soya milk can be made fresh every day if you grow your own soya beans. It is an easily digestible alkaline food and doctors recommend it for babies and adults with lactose intolerance. Compared to cows' milk it has more iron, no sodium, a sixth of the calcium, half the fat, half the calories, similar amounts of B vitamins, far fewer chemical residues, no cholesterol and equal protein.

YUBA

Yuba is an exceptionally delicious and highly nutritious food recommended in the East especially for pregnant women and nursing mothers. It contains

54 per cent pure protein and 33 per cent polyunsaturated fat. It is rightly considered a great delicacy. It can be made at home from soya milk.

You will need a *bain-marie* – a meat roasting tray and an inner container with a large surface area, such as a lasagne dish. Put the dish in the roasting tray and pour water into the tray. Set on the stove over gentle heat. When the water starts to steam, pour soya milk into the dish to a depth of about 1 inch (2.5cm). Heat until the milk is steaming.

When a skin forms on the milk, loosen it all round the edges with a wetted knife, then take a moistened chopstick, slip it underneath the skin and lift it out in one piece. (This is quite a delicate operation and, like pancake-making, may need some practice before you get it right.) Lay the yuba flat on a plate or a moistened bamboo mat to dry.

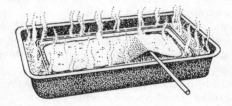

Repeat the process each time a skin forms on the soya milk, until the skin is not firm enough to lift off. Lay the yuba sheets like pancakes on top of each other to dry.

If you are not going to eat it straight away, yuba can be kept in the fridge in cling wrap, or deep-frozen.

WHEY

Whey is the liquid separated from the curds once the coagulant has been added during the production of tofu. The whey should not be wasted. It is a multi-purpose by-product of tofu. It contains protein, B vitamins and natural sugar. It can be used in making soups and bread. It can also be put in the washing machine because its high alkalinity combats grease. Other uses for whey are as shampoo, face cleanser and salad dressing. In the East it is sold as a washing-up liquid.

YUBA ROLLS

Serve these delicious rolls for a light lunch or supper. Quantities for the filling will depend on what size your yuba sheets turn out to be.

sheets of yuba
egg white

For filling I	Filling II
shredded lettuce	*mustard-and-cress*
shrimps	*grated carrot*
beansprouts	*cooked peas*
lemon juice	*pine nuts*
soy sauce	*soy sauce*

Combine the ingredients for the filling in a bowl. Divide between the sheets of yuba, roll up and seal with egg white. The rolls can be either steamed or deep-fried until crisp.

OKARA FIGGY BISCUITS

These high-fibre biscuits are crunchy and wholesome.

3 tablespoons honey
2 tablespoons oil
1 egg, beaten
2 oz (50g) dried figs, soaked in fruit tea until plump, chopped
1/2 teaspoon allspice
1/2 teaspoon salt (optional)
5 oz (150g) wholewheat flour
5 oz (150g) okara

Blend together the honey and oil, then add the egg. Mix in the remaining ingredients until well combined, then form into small balls and flatten into biscuits. Lay on a baking tray and bake at 400°F/200°C/Gas 6 for about 15 minutes until golden. They will be slightly soft. When they have cooled for a few minutes, put them on a wire rack to cool completely until crisp.

OKARA BANANA CAKE

Try this cake for breakfast for a change from a bran-based cereal.

2 oz (50g) polyunsaturated margarine
3 tablespoons molasses
2 eggs
2–3 mashed bananas
5 oz (150g) wholewheat flour
5 oz (150g) okara
2 teaspoons baking powder
1/2 teaspoon baking soda

Beat together the margarine and molasses, then beat in the eggs. Combine well with the bananas.

In another bowl, mix the dry ingredients together well.

Fold the dry ingredients into the banana mixture. Tip the batter into a greased and floured bread tin and bake at 350°F/180°C/Gas 4 for 1 hour, until a cocktail stick pushed into the cake comes out clean.

WHEY FACE CLEANSER

Keep some whey in a screw-topped bottle on the bathroom shelf and use in place of your regular cleanser. It is gentle and particularly good for greasy skins. Simply soak a cotton-wool pad in whey and stroke lightly across the face night and morning. You will find it an excellent make-up remover.

TOFU IN JAPAN

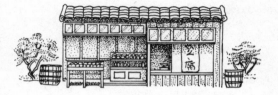

In Japan there is a tradition which regards skilled work and craftsmanship as a way of life rather than a job. The master craftsman fulfils himself through the act of labour rather than by his finished product. Losing himself to the rhythms of his work, he is at one with the tools of his trade and the material he is crafting. So it is with the tofu master.

An apprentice will serve with a master for a number of years. He will learn about hygiene and economy, and how not to waste natural resources such as heat and water. He will also be taught grace of movement, such as how to lift weights and how to stand most comfortably when performing certain tasks. Many young men become apprenticed to their fathers and eventually take over the family shop, but anyone setting up a new shop is given his master's name, rather like a coat-of-arms, to put on his shop sign and his tools.

One thing a master does not give away is his secret recipe – an apprentice has to learn this as a matter of instinct. The best tofu is not made scientifically, that is to say by relying entirely on weight, measures and exact timing. A master will take into account the quality of the beans, the purity of the water, the heat of the wood fire and the ambient temperature and humidity. He responds to his work not just with his brain, but with all his senses.

The tofu master and his wife get up before dawn to make tofu for breakfast shoppers, who arrive at about 7 or 8 a.m. They also sell deep-fried tofu, and many sell other breakfast foods besides. Miso, seaweed and dried mushrooms, for example. The rest of the day may be spent delivering tofu to restaurants, which do not usually make their own, or selling it from a trailer on the back of a bicycle. In summer chilled tofu is appreciated by the customers; in winter, hearty simmering tofu is preferred.

The tofu master and his wife pay scrupulous attention to their tools, often hand-crafted, and to the hygiene in the shop, which is usually quite a small room adjacent to their home with a sales window to the street. The shop has its own water supply, pumped from a well rather than from a tap. There will be large sinks for washing the equipment and unmoulding the tofu underwater, vats for soaking the beans and a grinder for producing the go.

The go is cooked in a massive cauldron over a wood fire and the soya milk is driven from it by a hydraulic press. The settling boxes, in which the tofu cakes are formed, are hand-made from wood.

The process of making tofu in a shop in Japan is exactly the same as you would make it at home, only on a larger scale.

JAPAN'S TOFU RESTAURANTS

Tofu is one of the most important ingredients in Japan's haute cuisine as well as in the everyday diet of the average Japanese. Whole restaurants specialise in tofu cookery. Some of the most famous have been owned and run by successive generations of the same family for over 400 years and offer up to 100 varieties of tofu at any given season.

In spring a dish of tofu might be garnished with a single cherry blossom; in summer it could be served chilled with a glowing orange lily, while in winter a picture-on-a-plate might use the virgin white of the tofu to symbolise snow. The Japanese take as much pleasure in the look of their food as in the taste of it. Each small dish in a series of courses is presented as a work of art, with the tofu and vegetables sliced and cut to create a symphony of colours, shapes, textures and flavours.

Japanese haute cuisine has two branches, and tofu

is used extensively in both of them. Zen Temple Cookery dates back to the 13th century, when monks in the Buddhist temples prepared food for visitors and pilgrims with tofu they had made in their monasteries. Tofu was the basis of their vegetarian diet and tofu restaurants are still to be found in or near many Zen temples today. Tea Ceremony Cuisine has developed from Zen Temple Cookery, and is highly sophisticated and very expensive. Tofu is to be found in about half the dishes on a Tea Ceremony menu.

The Japanese rate tofu highly as a food, and not just for its versatility and nutritive properties. To them it is a noble and dignified food – a simple wholesome thing produced from a bean by a craftsman. They honour this fact by taking as much care with the surroundings in which it is eaten as with the preparation of the food itself.

In a tofu restaurant the accent is on simplicity and elegance and the atmosphere is warm and peaceful, for all who eat together are treated as equals. Often there are several private dining rooms situated round a tranquil courtyard garden where a stream runs through an area of ornamental raked sand or smooth flat pebbles planted with bamboo. Inside the dining room, wood, stone and other natural materials instil harmony into the guests, who are invited to take off their shoes and sit on low rush seats, perhaps round a stone hearth. Here a hostess will invite them to select the tofu dishes of their choice, which she will then cook for them over live coals, while a cast-iron cauldron simmers above with water for tea.

JAPANESE COUNTRY-STYLE TOFU

Country-style tofu, as produced in the remote villages of Japan, is made in large blocks so firm that they can be wrapped in rice straw and tied with rope, like parcels, and carried by the rope without breaking.

Only hand-made tools are used in the production of this rustic tofu. The beans are grown in the surrounding fields and the water comes from deep wells and pure springs. Even the coagulant, nigari, is produced at home from unrefined sea salt. The beans are ground between hand-turned stones and cooked in an iron cauldron over a wood fire, which gives the tofu a delicate smoky flavour. Pressing takes place in a sack hung over a barrel – the idea is to let fine strands of okara through into the soya milk to make the tofu more substantial. Then the curds are pressed in a home-made box under a stone.

Country-style tofu is eaten up to three times a day by all the family in the winter, when snow stops work in the fields and allows more time for tofu-making. During the rest of the year it is eaten to commemorate festivals such as marriages, anniversaries and funerals, as well as religious occasions and the important events in the farming year. Gifts of tofu are always brought to housewarmings.

One of the favourite ways of eating country-style tofu is as *dengaku*. The portions of tofu are spread with miso, also made on the farm, then speared with wooden skewers and grilled over live coals. This delicious dish is found in many city restaurants.

Japanese Sukiyaki

Sukiyaki, like fondue, is an occasion as well as a meal. The guests sit round a hot plate or other heat source and, using chopsticks, cook their own food in a large pan, first dipping it in raw egg. The cooked food is then dipped in sauce and eaten with noodles (rice if you prefer).

14 oz (400g) dried noodles
4 small eggs
3–4 tablespoons vegetable oil

For the sukiyaki
4 large leaves of Chinese cabbage
1 lb (450g) spinach
1 bunch spring onions, cut into short lengths
8 oz (225g) mushrooms, sliced
1 medium aubergine, halved lengthways then sliced
8 oz (225g) tofu, cubed

For the sauce
4 fl oz (100ml) soy sauce
8 fl oz (225ml) dashi (see page 58) or vegetable stock, incorporating the spinach juices
2 tablespoons runny honey
3 tablespoons sherry

First make the spinach rolls, which form part of the sukiyaki. Blanch the Chinese cabbage leaves, drain and dry on absorbent paper. Steam the spinach for a couple of minutes until tender. Do not throw the water in the pan away. Chop the spinach and divide between the leaves and roll up tightly. Allow to cool, then cut into ½ inch (1 cm) slices.

Arrange all the ingredients for the sukiyaki on a large platter. Mix all the sauce ingredients together in a bowl. Cook the noodles for 10 minutes in boiling water, drain and place in a serving bowl.

Heat the oil in the pan over a heat source on the table. Each guest will need two bowls and a pair of chopsticks. Invite everyone to break an egg into one bowl and whisk it with chopsticks. When the oil is hot, the guests can help themselves to the sukiyaki ingredients, dipping them in beaten egg before cooking them. Offer the sauce and noodles.

Serves 4

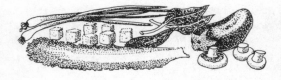

STUFFED FRIED TOFU POUCHES

Mixtures of finely chopped vegetables or shrimps and cooked rice are ideal for stuffing tofu. The pouches can be any size from about 2 inches (5cm) square. Bigger ones can be filled with more substantial ingredients, such as a whole raw egg, which will take about 2 minutes' deep-frying to cook, and looks spectacular when cut open.

To make 8 pouches, slice an 8 oz (225g) rectangle of tofu in half through its narrowest edges so that you have two slim rectangles of the same size as the original block. Then cut each one of these in half lengthways. Pour boiling water over them, then drain and dry on absorbent paper. Cut each in half across the middle, and open the cut edge to form a pouch.

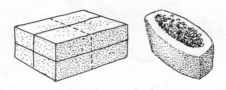

Stuff with a mixture of cooked rice, sesame seeds and chopped cooked shiitake mushrooms (a heaped teaspoonful should be enough, depending on the size of the pouch). Shiitake can be bought fresh in Oriental grocers, but are most often available dried in 1 oz (25g) packets (containing about 10 mushrooms). They are known as Japanese tree mushrooms, because they are cultivated by injecting fungus into the soft bark of water-soaked tree trunks. If you buy them dried, they will need to be soaked in water for about an hour, then cooked in their soaking liquid with a little soy sauce added, until the liquid has evaporated.

Seal pouches with egg white, deep- or shallow-fry until hot through and golden. Serve straight away.

Deep-Fried Tofu

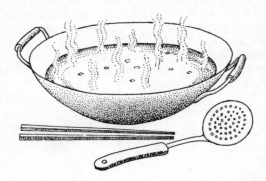

This is the most popular way of eating tofu in the Orient. In Japan, deep-fried tofu is called agé. The beauty of agé is that the hot oil is not absorbed into it, it just crisps the outside.

Marinate the tofu cubes or slices before frying, or serve with a piquant sauce and a garnish of spring onions or shredded baby leeks. The marinade can be soy sauce on its own, or a combination of ingredients as suggested below. Lightly score the surface of the tofu for maximum penetration.

Another idea is to roll the tofu in sesame seeds, or flour with a little cayenne pepper or other seasoning added, before frying. Alternatively, coat it in a batter flavoured with soy or chilli sauce.

The following are delicious combinations that can be used as marinades or sauces for 4 oz (100g) tofu cubes.

2 tablespoons soy sauce
½ inch (1 cm) ginger, grated
1 spring onion, chopped

1 teaspoon tandoori paste
2½ tablespoons lemon juice

1 tablespoon miso
1 tablespoon tahini

1½ tablespoons chilli sauce (bottled –
   an entirely natural product)
1 tablespoon horseradish sauce
1 teaspoon tomato concentrate

1 tablespoon tahini
1 tablespoon oil
1 tablespoon soy sauce

1 clove garlic, crushed
1 tablespoon sherry
1 tablespoon oil
1 tablespoon soy sauce

1 tablespoon peanut butter
2 tablespoons oil
pinch cayenne pepper

½ inch (1 cm) ginger, grated
1 clove garlic, crushed
1½ tablespoons oil
1 tablespoon lemon juice

TOFU IN INDONESIA

Eating tofu in Indonesia is a much more hectic experience than eating it in Japan. In Indonesia tofu is called *tahu* and prepared freshly every day in about 11,000 small shops. Often it is dyed yellow in turmeric or gardenia flowers.

A favourite way of eating tahu is to do so while on the move. Tahu sellers stand on station platforms and run along the corridors in trains, or sell it in the market place, deep-fried with hot chilli sauce. It is also enjoyed pickled in soya bean paste – a relative of miso – and as tofu chips. For this last delicacy, the tofu is sliced, lightly salted and left in the sun to dry, before being dipped in rice flour and deep-fried.

The process of making tahu in Indonesia is particularly economical, as the go is cooked over a fire of rice husks and not wood, and the coagulant is not nigari but fermenting whey from the previous day's batch of tahu. Appropriately enough, the starter whey is called *ibu* or *biang*, meaning mother.

TEMPEH

Indonesia is also the home of tempeh, another food in the soya family and a close relation of tofu. Tempeh is a cake of soya beans bound by a mycelium of rhizopus mold. Like cheese, it is a fermented food and its flavour is reminiscent of Brie or Camembert with perhaps a hint of mushrooms and nuts.

Though it can be eaten uncooked, the best way of serving tempeh is sliced and fried until crisp. It is delicious cooked like this and eaten as burgers, in sandwiches, as croûtons and in stir-fries.

Tempeh is 19.5 per cent protein and is the world's richest known source of vitamin B_{12}, which can be in short supply in the diet of vegetarians who don't eat dairy produce. It is an excellent diet food, and has only 39 calories per ounce (25g). Because it has been fermented it is very easily digestible.

In Indonesia there are about 30 varieties of tempeh, because the soya beans can be combined with peanuts, rice, millet or wheat to give different flavours, or these latter can be fermented on their own without using soya beans.

To make soya tempeh, soya beans are rinsed, brought just to the boil, then soaked overnight in the water. In the morning they are dehulled. If it is a small operation, this can be done by rubbing them between the palms of the hands, otherwise the beans are trampled underfoot like grapes in bamboo baskets. They are then cooked till tender, drained and cooled. They are mixed with a spore culture starter which has been grown on soya beans layered with hibiscus leaves. They are then incubated for 24 hours and packed in bags or tins.

Tempeh can be eaten at various stages of ripeness, just like Camembert. It gets softer and more pungent as it ripens. It is most often bought frozen at an early stage of ripeness and should be defrosted and stored in the fridge until ready.

SATAY TOFU

These Indonesian kebabs can be cooked on a barbecue or under the grill.

8 oz (225g) tofu, cubed

For the marinade
1 tablespoon soya oil
1 tablespoon honey
1 tablespoon sherry
1 tablespoon soy sauce
1 teaspoon tomato concentrate
1 clove garlic, crushed
1 green chilli, seeds removed, sliced

For the peanut sauce
4 tablespoons peanut butter
2 tablespoons oil
1 tablespoon lemon juice
1 clove garlic, crushed
soy sauce and *molasses to taste*

Combine the ingredients for the marinade, coat the tofu cubes in it and leave, covered, in the fridge for a couple of hours. Combine the ingredients for the sauce.

Thread the tofu cubes on to wooden skewers and barbecue or grill for about 2 minutes each side. Serve with the peanut sauce.

Serves 4

NASI GORENG WITH TOFU

This Indonesian dish is best cooked in a wok. Cooked or semi-cooked ingredients can be pushed up the sides of the wok and kept hot while other ingredients are added and cooked.

4 tablespoons oil
14 oz (400g) cooked brown rice
2 carrots and *2 courgettes, cut into matchsticks*
4 oz (100g) mushrooms, sliced
4 spring onions, sliced
8 oz (225g) tofu, cubed
4 eggs, beaten

For the spice paste
1 medium onion, chopped
½ teaspoon each chilli powder and *cumin*
1 clove garlic, crushed
1 teaspoon honey

First make the spice paste by liquidizing the ingredients with ¼ pint (150ml) water until smooth.

Heat half the oil in a wok, add the paste and cook, stirring, for 1 minute. Add the rice and stir-fry until hot. Then push the rice up the sides of the wok, add the remaining oil and stir-fry the vegetables for 3 minutes. Stir in the rice, add the tofu and the beaten eggs. Continue to cook for a couple of minutes, stirring without breaking the tofu, until the egg has set.

Serves 4

TOFU IN CHINA

In China, tofu is called *doufu*. Apart from the fresh variety described in this book, which the empresses of the Ch'ing Dynasty used to eat to improve their complexions, the Chinese enjoy some unusual tofu specialities. *Choudoufu*, or smelly tofu, was invented by chance in Peking in 1669, when a tofu master made more than he could sell and to stop his product going rancid – it was already fermenting briskly – threw some salt and spices into the vat. To his surprise the smelly tofu was an instant hit with his customers and made his fame and fortune. Choudoufu is made today by fermenting tofu for two weeks in a broth made of soya beans, mushrooms, bamboo shoots and rice wine. It is then deep-fried in tea oil until crisp and stuffed with a hot spicy sauce. It looks mouldy and the people of Hunan province say it tastes delicious.

In Hubei in northern China they make *dongdoufu* by leaving tofu outside overnight in the snow. It freezes and becomes spongy, with the texture of meat. This is the original forerunner of soya protein, which can be made at home in the freezer. The Chinese eat it braised or stir-fried with vegetables.

There is a charming story about dongdoufu, which says that it was invented by a Daoist monk to feed the pilgrims who had journeyed to his monastery. In despair at not having enough food to give them, he left his tofu out in the snow. In the morning it had turned into dongdoufu – and such a quantity of it that there was enough to feed everyone.

In Anhui province the specialities are *maodoufu* – hairy tofu, which is covered with white mould; and *meidoufu* – mildewed tofu. Both are pan-fried to bring out the mouldy aroma.

STIR-FRIED TOFU

With a wok or frying pan, a nutritious meal takes only a few minutes to prepare. A simple Chinese stir-fry is equal quantities of beansprouts or shredded baby leeks and tofu cubes, with a crushed clove of garlic and a dash of soy sauce.

For a mixed vegetable dish you will need about 7 oz (200g) vegetables and 2 oz (50g) tofu per person. The vegetables should be trimmed and finely sliced or chopped. Choose vegetables that need minimal cooking and make a good contrast of shapes, colours and flavours. The tofu can be marinated in one of the dressings on page 49 and added when the vegetables are almost done.

MISO

Miso, along with tofu and rice, is one of the foods eaten at least once a day in the average Japanese household. Like tofu, it is made from soya beans – miso is in fact a fermented soya bean paste. It can be spread on slices of tofu and grilled to make one of Japan's favourite national dishes, dengaku, but it is most often used to make a stock or vegetarian gravy with a delicious hearty flavour. A tablespoon of miso can be creamed in a cup with two or three times as much hot water and poured over a vegetable and tofu dish to make a sauce, or added to dashi, a Japanese bouillon, to make miso soup.

Miso soup is the traditional Japanese breakfast. Each household has its own special recipe, but it is popularly eaten with tofu cubes floating in it and accompanied by a bowl of rice and perhaps some salt-pickled vegetables and plums.

Miso soup is attributed by the Japanese with near-miraculous properties. They drink it to cure hangovers, to neutralize an acid stomach, purge the body of nicotine, cure colds, clear the skin and build up resistance to disease. Miso contains a substance called zybicolin, which is known to attract, absorb and discharge radioactivity from the body, a fact which was discovered after Nagasaki was bombed. Miso soup is on sale in vending machines in offices and factories and served daily in police canteens – it is especially recommended for traffic policemen, who are subjected to very high levels of pollution.

Like yoghurt, miso is a live food containing bacilli that effectively combat poisons in the body and cleanse the gut. Bulgarian nonagenarians claim that yoghurt has given them long life and health, and Japanese nonagenarians claim the same thing for miso.

Miso has been eaten in Japan since the seventh century. Today it is made by 2,500 master craftsmen across the country and treated with the reverence – and the relish – accorded in the West to fine wines and cheeses.

The traditional farmhouse way of making miso is to cook soya beans, then crush them, press them into a ball and roll it up in rice straw. This is then hung up indoors over the stove or outside under the eaves of the house for about a month to 'catch' wild mold spores. When the ball is covered with a growth of mold, the beans are pounded into a pulp, turned into crocks, mixed with salt and water and left to ferment for at least a year.

In the thousands of miso shops to be found in Japan miso is made in huge cedar wood vats that hold 50 gallons and are anything up to 150 years old. There are 40 or 50 varieties of miso displayed in smaller kegs in the shop and available for tasting. They vary in colour, according to the exact ingredients and the fermenting time, from red to brown and black, with meaty, hearty flavours.

More recently yellow and beige types of miso have been developed. They are sweet and nutty and tend to be used in the cooking of lighter foods and desserts. Rice or barley can be added to the beans to produce another whole spectrum of flavours.

Miso is often used for pickling, and a popular new variety is finger-lickin' miso, with contains vegetable chunks.

Miso-making at home is on the increase in Japan, and in America you can now buy starter kits. The Japanese have a saying that anyone boasting about the achievements is showing off his home-made miso – perhaps this will soon be a common saying in the West too.

DASHI

Dashi is the traditional Japanese stock made with seaweed and dried fish. It forms the basis for many dishes, including miso soup. You can buy dashi in sachets like tea bags from Oriental specialist shops, and for a truly authentic taste you can make it yourself from scratch.

1½ pints (1 litre) water
1 oz (25g) kombo (dried kelp)
1 oz (25g) katsuobushi (flaked dried bonito – tuna fish)

Put the water on to heat and drop the kombo into it. Just before it boils, fish out the kombo with a slotted spoon. Add a cup of cold water and the bonito and bring back to the boil. Allow to boil for 2 minutes, then remove from the heat and strain.

Two Miso Soups

These are best made with dashi, but you could use vegetable stock cubes instead. It is important not to continue cooking after you have added the miso, as this would kill the bacilli. This soup is so popular in Japan that the telephone corporation offers a dial-a-miso-soup-of-the-day service.

1½ pints (1 litre) dashi
8 oz (225g) tofu, diced
2 tablespoons miso
spring onions, chopped, to garnish

Bring the dashi to the boil, drop in the tofu and simmer for 3 minutes. Put the miso in a cup and add a ladleful of dashi. Cream to a paste, return to the soup pan and stir to mix. Pour into soup bowls and serve garnished with spring onions.

Eat the vegetables and tofu with chopsticks and drink the soup steaming hot straight from the bowl.

1 small onion, diced
1–2 carrots, grated
1½ pints (1 litre) dashi
6 oz (175g) tofu, diced
2 tablespoons miso

Simmer the vegetables in the dashi for 5 minutes, then add the tofu. Cream the miso in a cup with a ladleful of dashi and return to the soup. Stir to mix, then serve.

OTHER TITLES IN THE SERIES

The Little Green Avocado Book
The Little Garlic Book
The Little Pepper Book
The Little Lemon Book
The Little Apple Book
The Little Strawberry Book
The Little Mustard Book
The Little Honey Book
The Little Nut Book
The Little Mushroom Book
The Little Bean Book
The Little Rice Book
The Little Tea Book
The Little Coffee Book
The Little Chocolate Book
The Little Curry Book
The Little Mediterranean Food Book
The Little Exotic Vegetable Book
The Little Exotic Fruit Book
The Little Yoghurt Book
The Little Breakfast Book
The Little Egg Book
The Little Potato Book